Schools Around the World

by Ellen Lawrence

Ruby Tuesday Books

Published in 2026 by Ruby Tuesday Books Ltd.

Editor: Mark J. Sachner
Design & Production: Emma Randall & Tammy West

Photo credits:
Alamy: Cover (Stefan Ember), 7 (Andrey Kekyalyaynen), 8 (Boaz Rottem), 10L (Ton Koene), 11BR (E. D. Torial), 14 (Cavan Images), 16 (Simon Price), 19 (dpa picture alliance), 20 (Jeffrey Isaac Greenberg); Corbis: 5TL; FLPA: 11L, 12–13, 17; Getty Images: 15; Shutterstock: 4 (Pavel Svoboda Photography), 5BL (photopoems), 6L (Chantal de Bruijne), 6R (bodom), 8–9 (Altrendo Images/Ana Flasker), 10C (Westock Productions), 10R (Ground Picture), 11TR (arindambanerjee), 18 (Quetions 123), 21 (Rumbo a lo desconocido); Superstock: 5R.

Library of Congress Control Number: 2024948737

Hardback ISBN 978-1-78856-543-1
Paperback ISBN 978-1-78856-544-8
ePub ISBN 978-1-78856-545-5

Published in Minneapolis, MN
Printed in the United States

www.rubytuesdaybooks.com

The picture on the front cover of this book shows a classroom of children at school in India.

CONTENTS

Words shown in bold in the text are explained in the glossary.

All the places in this book are shown on the map on page 22.

It's Time for School!

It's morning, and all over the world children are heading off to school.

Walking to school in India

A school bus in New York City

On a school day in the United States and Canada, millions of children ride to school on yellow buses.

These students in Myanmar travel to and from school by boat.

A small, crowded school bus in Indonesia

Welcome to Our Classroom

Kids spend their days in classrooms, but not all classrooms look the same.

In Tanzania, these Maasai children study in a classroom with walls made out of branches.

It's very hot in India, so these children learn in a classroom that helps them keep cool.

In Russia, classrooms are decorated with balloons for the first day of the **term** in September. Children bring flowers for their teachers and wear their best clothes.

A Floating School

Some children in Cambodia go to schools that float!

The children live on Tonlé Sap Lake.

Thousands of families live on the lake in houseboats and floating houses.

Floating school

Some schools won't let very young students come to school until they have learned to swim. Then it is safe for them to travel in the boats with their older friends.

To get to school, the children paddle small boats from their homes to their schools.

Our School Day

At school, kids read and write and study math and science.

These Xingu (sheen-GOO) children in the Amazon rain forest are reading a book together.

Some children work on computers and tablets.

This girl in India does her schoolwork on a chalkboard.

Children have fun making art.

These kids on the Falkland Islands have painted pictures of large seabirds called albatrosses. The birds come to the islands to lay eggs and raise their chicks.

We sing, make music, and dance.

We see our friends and favorite teachers.

A Library on a Camel

Many people in Kenya, in Africa, are **nomads** who move from place to place with their animals.

Their small villages, or camps, are usually far from towns.

The kids who live in these traveling villages still like to choose books from a library.

So the library comes to them on the back of a camel!

The camel library

A librarian, library assistants, and a camel herder travel with three camels. The animals carry about 200 books between them. The books are laid out on a mat on the ground so readers can make their choices.

Ready for Earthquakes

Japan is a country that has many **earthquakes** that can damage buildings.

Japanese children hiding under their desks

Once a month, most Japanese schools have an earthquake drill.

Children practice hiding under their desks to keep safe from falling walls or ceilings.

Buildings that are damaged by an earthquake may catch fire. During a drill, children practice taking different escape routes from their school. They also prepare for fires by wearing padded, fireproof hoods.

Going on a Class Trip

Many kids get to do learning outside of their classrooms.

These children in England are on a class trip to a farm.

They are learning how sheep and cattle are raised for meat.

These students in Kenya are visiting a center for orphaned baby elephants.

The babies' mothers were killed by hunters called **poachers.**

In Africa, thousands of adult elephants are killed by poachers each year. The animals are killed for their tusks, which are used to make jewelry and ornaments. During trips to the center, kids learn about protecting elephants.

A School in a Tent

Every year, thousands of people have to leave their homes because of war or natural disasters.

A refugee camp in Syria

These people become **refugees.**

Many find safety in a refugee camp, where they live in tents or other small homes.

At a camp, children may go to school in a tent classroom.

These children are having a math lesson in a tent classroom. The students and their teacher are refugees who had to leave their homes because of war.

A tent classroom in Syria

No Time for School

Many children cannot go to school because they have to work.

They may earn just a few cents for a day's work.

This money helps their families pay for food and medical care.

Thankfully, many people are trying to help working children.

This girl in Peru earns money selling gum on the street.

In Cambodia, some children work on garbage dumps, collecting items that can be sold to recycling companies.

One thing that can be changed to help working children is to make bosses pay adult workers higher wages. If parents can earn more money, their children won't have to work.

Welcome to My World

United States
Page 5

England
Page 16

Germany
Page 11

Syria
Pages 18–19

Russia
Page 7

India
Pages 4, 6, and 10

Japan
Pages 14–15

Canada
Page 10

North America

Europe

Asia

Africa

Haiti
Page 11

Cambodia
Pages 8–9 and 21

South America

Australia

Brazil
Page 10

Tanzania
Page 6

India
Front cover

Indonesia
Page 5

Peru
Page 20

Falkland Islands
Page 11

Kenya
Pages 12–13 and 17

Myanmar
Page 5

GLOSSARY

earthquake
A sudden shaking caused by underground movements in Earth's outer layer, or crust.

nomad
A person who regularly moves from one area to another and does not live in one place all the time.

poacher
A person who breaks the law by killing an animal or taking it from its natural habitat.

refugee
A person who has been forced to leave their home to escape danger and needs to be protected.

term
A period of time, which usually lasts for several weeks or months, during which children must go to school. Between each school term there are holiday and summer breaks.

INDEX